The Baby's Catalogue

Janet and Allan Ahlberg

An Atlantic Monthly Press Book

Little, Brown and Company
Boston

Library of Congress Catalog Card No. 82-9928

Second Printing

ISBN 0-316-02037-0

Atlantic–Little, Brown Books
are published by
Little, Brown and Company
in association with
The Atlantic Monthly Press

Published in Great Britain by Kestrel, Penguin Books Ltd

Printed in Great Britain by William Clowes Ltd

Contents

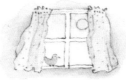

For Jessica

 # Babies

Dads

Moms

Mornings

High Chairs

Breakfasts

Toys

Teddy Bear	Blocks	Rattle	Top
Tricycle	Doll	Car	Ducks
Frog	Wagon	Elephant	Ball

Brothers and Sisters

Carriages

Swings

Diapers

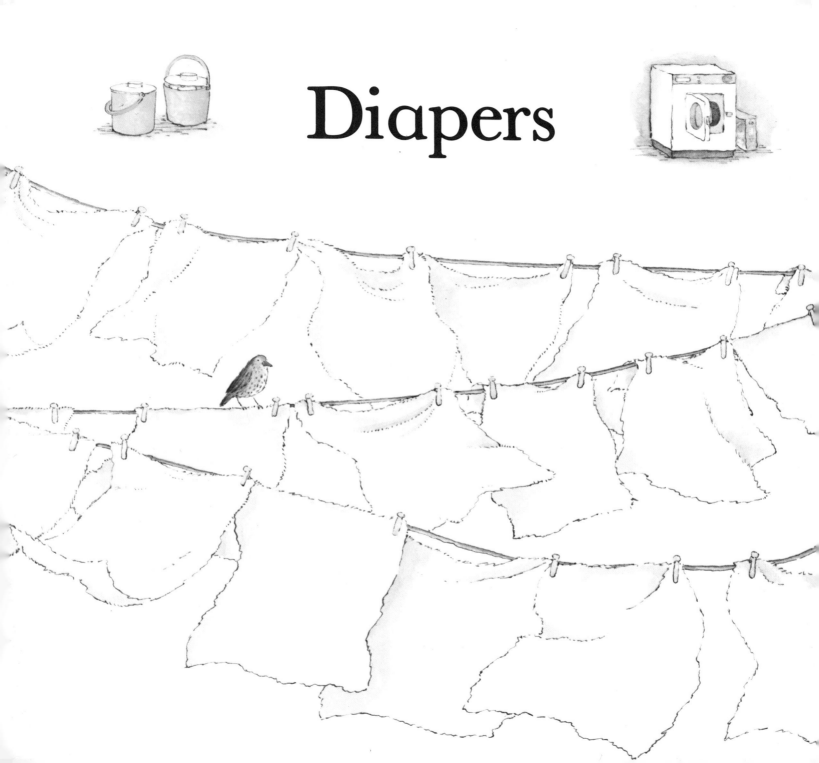

Bouncing

Piggyback

Catching

Games

Climbing

Peeka-

boo!

Shopping

Fruit

Cans

Baby Things

Sausages

Boxes

Lunches

Gardens

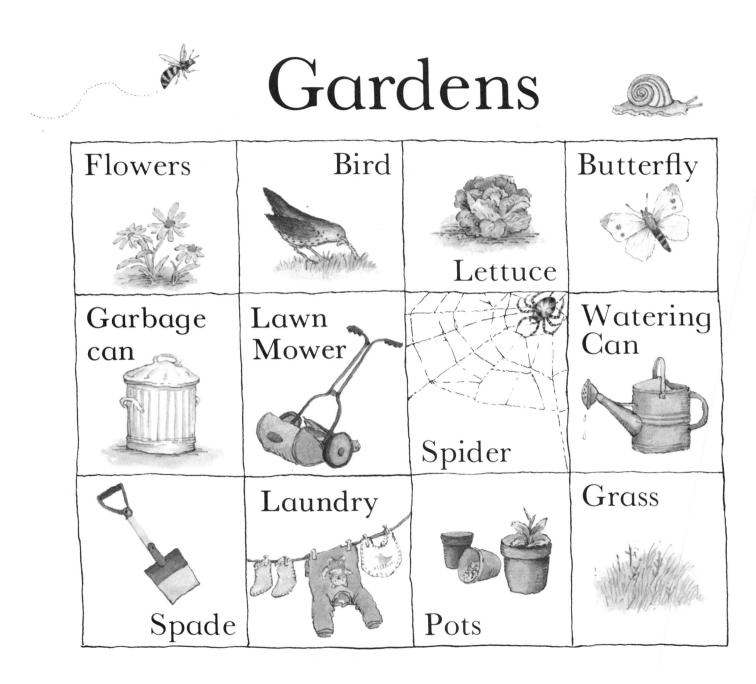

Flowers	Bird	Lettuce	Butterfly
Garbage can	Lawn Mower	Spider	Watering Can
Spade	Laundry	Pots	Grass

Wading Pool

Sandbox

Accidents

Mirrors

Pets

Dog

Hamster

Frog

Rabbit

Parakeet

Goldfish

Cat

Mouse

Kittens

Caterpillar

Dog

Guinea Pig

Ants

Suppers

Cups

Pots

Bread

Salad

Cakes

Books

Baths

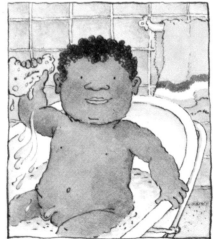

 # Bedtimes

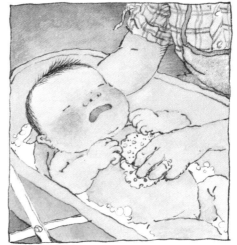

Moms and Dads

Babies

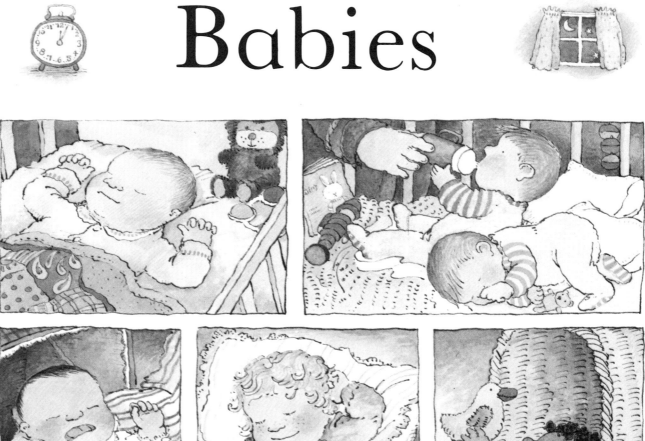

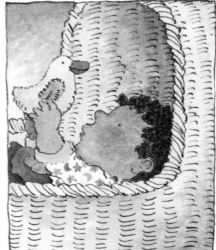

The End